Monster Machines

# Aircraft Carriers

By Kenny Allen

**Gareth Stevens**
Publishing

Please visit our website, www.garethstevens.com. For a free color catalog of all our high-quality books, call toll free 1-800-542-2595 or fax 1-877-542-2596.

**Library of Congress Cataloging-in-Publication Data**

Allen, Kenny, 1971-
Aircraft carriers / Kenny Allen.
      p. cm. — (Monster machines)
Includes index.
ISBN 978-1-4339-7160-0 (pbk.)
ISBN 978-1-4339-7161-7 (6-pack)
ISBN 978-1-4339-7159-4 (library binding)
1. Aircraft carriers—Juvenile literature. I. Title.
V874.A45 2012
623.825′5—dc23

                                        2011043220

First Edition

Published in 2013 by
**Gareth Stevens Publishing**
111 East 14th Street, Suite 349
New York, NY 10003

Designer: Daniel Hosek
Editor: Greg Roza

Photo credits: Cover, pp. 1, 5, 11 StockTrek/Getty Images; borders, p. 9 Shutterstock.com; p. 7 AFP/Getty Images; p. 13 Getty Images; p. 15 Ingram Publishing/Thinkstock.com; p. 17 U.S. Navy/Getty Images; p. 19 Check Six/Getty Images; p. 21 Sandy Huffaker/Getty Images.

Printed in the United States of America

CPSIA compliance information: Batch #CS12GS: For further information contact Gareth Stevens, New York, New York at 1-800-542-2595.

# Contents

**Boldface** words appear in the glossary.

## Giants of the Sea

The aircraft carrier is one of the largest ships ever made. An aircraft carrier needs to be big enough to carry an air force. This monster machine is about as long as a skyscraper is tall!

5

Aircraft carriers **transport** jets and **soldiers** all over the world. The largest aircraft carriers carry up to 100 jets. More than 5,000 soldiers might be aboard an aircraft carrier at one time!

## Steel Ship

An aircraft carrier is made of steel. The top is very wide, but the part under the water is much narrower. Inside are levels called decks. There are more than 4,000 rooms on these decks.

9

## On the Flight Deck

The top of an aircraft carrier is called the flight deck. It's where jets take off and land. Many soldiers work on the flight deck. Some make sure pilots are safe. Others take care of the jets.

11

Jets on aircraft carriers need help taking off and landing. During takeoffs, **catapults** get jets up to speed very quickly. When landing, jets have hooks that grab onto strong cables to slow them down quickly.

# The Island

The island is a tower where officers watch the action on the flight deck. Other soldiers help steer the ship. **Radar** dishes on the island help the crew find the enemy. Radio **antennas** allow officers to talk to pilots.

BEWARE OF PROPS ROTORS
JET INTAKE AND EXHAUST

15

## In the Hangar

Beneath the flight deck is a large space called the hangar. A hangar is big enough to store more than 60 jets. Several giant elevators move jets between the hangar and the flight deck.

# Power!

An aircraft carrier's powerful engines are on the lowest deck. They create energy to turn four giant **propellers**. The engines also make electricity to power lights and machinery throughout the aircraft carrier.

19

# City at Sea

An aircraft carrier is like a floating city. Soldiers live and work on the middle decks. Those decks have a post office, hospital, barber shop, and stores. Aircraft carriers even have their own newspapers and television studios!

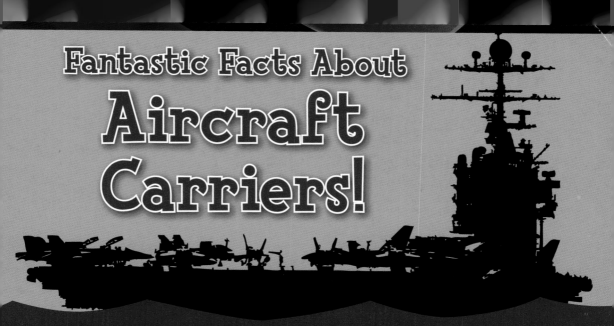

# Fantastic Facts About Aircraft Carriers!

- The biggest aircraft carrier is nearly 4 football fields long.

- An island is as tall as a 15-story building.

- Jets can take off from or land on an aircraft carrier once every 25 seconds.

- An aircraft carrier has two anchors. Each anchor weighs as much as 6 elephants.

# Glossary

**antenna:** a metal rod used to send and receive radio messages

**catapult:** a machine that throws something with great force

**propeller:** paddle-like parts on a ship that spin in the water to move the ship forward

**radar:** a way of using radio waves to find distant objects

**soldier:** someone in the military

**transport:** to move people or things from one place to another

# For More Information

## Books

Doeden, Matt. *Aircraft Carriers*. Minneapolis, MN: Lerner Publications, 2006.

Peppas, Lynn. *Aircraft Carriers: Runways at Sea*. New York, NY: Crabtree Publishing, 2012.

Tagliaferro, Linda. *Who Lands Planes on a Ship? Working on an Aircraft Carrier*. Chicago, IL: Raintree, 2011.

## Websites

### How Aircraft Carriers Work
*www.howstuffworks.com/aircraft-carrier.htm*
Read more about aircraft carriers, and see amazing pictures of them being built and at sea.

### Intrepid Sea, Air and Space Museum
*www.intrepidmuseum.org*
Learn about the famous aircraft carrier the USS *Intrepid*, and plan a trip to see it in New York City.

# Index